NEW BEGINNINGS

New Beginnings
Kawana Hibbert-Quinn
Yolanda Hibbert

Copyright © 2024 by Kawana Hibbert-Quinn

ISBN 979-8-89383-932-6

NEW BEGINNINGS

EMBRACING WHAT'S NEW TO COME

KAWANA HIBBERT - QUINN

WITH

YOLANDA HIBBERT

CONTENTS

I want to dedicate this book to my husband, Kenyatta, and my boys, Emanee and Isaiah. My God and boys inspired this book, and my husband provided the motivation I needed to complete it. Additionally, I cannot forget to mention my niece, Yolanda, who significantly shaped this book. I also empathize with those who, like me, may have a story to tell but struggle to express it. I refer to these individuals as "silent writers." To all the silent writers out there, I want to encourage you to keep writing and not give up, regardless of any obstacles you may face.

PROLOGUE

eet Aaron, a young boy who has just moved from Chicago to Florida. This new experience is both exciting and nerve-racking for him as he leaves behind everything and everyone he knows.

However, he is enthusiastic about exploring his new surroundings and seeing how he adjusts to life in the Sunshine State. Despite the significant change, we believe he will rise to the challenge. Come along on Aaron's journey and witness his personal growth.

CHAPTER I
STARTING OVER

We must develop and maintain the capacity to forgive. He who is devoid of the power to forgive is devoid of the power to love. There is some good in the worst of us and some evil in the best of us. When we discover this, we are less prone to hate our enemies.
– Martin Luther King Jr.

Hi there. My name is Aaron, and I recently moved to Florida. It can be tough to make new friends, especially since most of our communication is through screens. I'm in the final year of middle school, so it's a bit of a challenge, but I'm excited for this new chapter.

Although I'm a bit nervous, I'm confident I can handle it. My mom has been my incredible support system since my dad passed away, and I'm thankful for her. While it's nice to have the latest fashion and designer clothes, I'm aware that true friendships aren't about material things. I'm excited to meet new people and have a fantastic year. Although I may feel anxious, I trust myself and know I'll be okay on the first day of school. Whenever I have these feelings, I write them down in my journal.

JOURNAL ENTRY 1

Starting over in a new school and state is challenging, especially without my dad. Last year was tough for my family as my father passed away from COVID. I'm sure many others have also struggled to adapt to the crisis we have been experiencing. My mom is the only one who can help and guide me through this new journey. I want a great year, but it isn't easy since I haven't met any kids my age since moving to Florida. Unfortunately, we live in a small community where people are not very friendly. I miss my dad terribly and wish he were here to help me adjust to these situations. It's possible we wouldn't have moved if he were still alive. I hope the school is better than the neighborhood, but I'm not too optimistic. Despite all this, there is a silver lining—my mom is making my favorite meal tonight: lasagna and garlic bread.

After dinner, I wanted to share my feelings with my mother. Unfortunately, she was on a work call and couldn't give me her attention, leaving me feeling isolated. It reminded me how much I miss my father, who I used to confide in when I felt frustrated and anxious. I felt discouraged and retreated to my room. But then my younger brother, Emmanuel, startled me by jumping out from behind a wall. He was boasting about his day ahead, saying he would make new friends and have a better teacher than me. His behavior was aggravating, and I pushed him away, asking him to leave me alone. Emmanuel, four years younger than me, enjoys provoking me. He's adapting to our recent move better than I am. Eventually, he left to play his piano loudly, further irritating me. After an hour, our mother came in and reminded us it was time for bed and to wrap up our activities.

Mom mentioned that you wanted to talk to me, Aaron. Don't worry, I'm doing okay. I've been thinking about talking to my mom, but I don't want to add more stress to her plate. She's already keeping a roof over our heads and food on the table. I'm feeling agitated inside, and journaling hasn't been helpful. I know she's still grieving the loss of my dad and cries herself to sleep at night, but she's doing her best to be strong for Emmanuel and me. If you ever need a listening ear, know I am always here. My nightly routine involves receiving a goodnight kiss from my mother and reciting bedtime prayers and daily affirmations before retiring to my bedroom.

"Good morning, good morning, good morning, it's time to rise and shine. Get up! Get up, you sleepy heads. Get up, get up, get out of bed! Good morning, Aaron; good morning, Mom; let's get up and get ready. I will have breakfast ready in 15 minutes. Don't forget to say your affirmations." I get out of bed and pull out my clothes for school. I start saying my daily affirmations:

"I am smart."

"I am enough."

"I am an amazing person. Today, I am a leader."

"All my problems have a solution."

"There is no one better to thank than myself. I am intelligent."

"I am powerful."

I start my morning strong with affirmations that my parents taught both Emmanuel and me. Following this, I efficiently prepare for school by taking a shower, brushing my teeth, and dressing confidently. Once I'm ready, I confidently head to the kitchen, where Emmanuel is already enjoying breakfast.

Emmanuel asked Aaron whether he had recited his affirmations as part of his daily routine. However, Aaron questioned the relevance of Emmanuel's inquiry to his personal life.

"Mom, Aaron didn't say his affirmations this morning. You're such a baby; eat your food so we can go."

After breakfast, we grabbed our backpacks and headed to the car. Mom was dropping us off at school.

"Do you guys have more than one mask in your backpacks?"

"Yes, Mom," we responded.

"Are you ready for what the day has to offer you?"

Emmanuel and I gave different responses when Mom asked if we were ready. She wondered why we weren't prepared. I explained that I was starting over in a new place and didn't know anyone. I am so frustrated and scared by this new start, but I won't tell Mom. Mom reassured me that I would make friends quickly because I am a great kid. She encouraged me to make a difference and have a positive attitude. Emmanuel asked, "What about him?" Mom said he always has a fun-filled day and is ready for change. She wished us both a great day and reminded us to put a smile on someone's face. We thanked her and got out of the car, excited to start our first day at Henry Allen K-8 School.

As Emmanuel's screeches echoed through the ominous hallway, I knew our thrilling adventure was about to begin. Guided by various signs, we headed to our designated classrooms. Being an eighth grader, my classroom was located in the West Wing, while Emmanuel, a fourth grader, belonged to the East Wing. After we parted ways, I strolled down my hallway. I observed themes such as "Minecraft," "Harry Potter," TikTok, and YouTube. Although the hallway seemed never-ending, like the Twilight Zone, I didn't let it intimidate me. Eventually, I reached my classroom door and confidently introduced myself to Mrs. Quinn, who greeted me pleasantly. I sat at the soccer table, as I am a player, hoping to make some new friends this year. Already seated at the table were two boys, Connor and Kingston, who appeared to be amicable. Mrs. Quinn closed the door and instructed us to take a sheet of paper from the center of the table, which contained our class schedule filled with various activities and tasks. I was excited to start the day and make the most of this new opportunity.

Today is going to be a long day. I've noticed that I pick up on the lessons faster than Connor, but Kingston is advanced. We work well together as a group, and I'm impressed by our teamwork. Although we're not friends, I can see a friendship forming soon. Lunchtime has arrived, and I'm so hungry. As we entered the cafeteria, I noticed a foul smell that seemed to be coming from day-old broccoli. It's disappointing because we have to wear masks all day, and the one time we can take them off, the smell is unbearable. I get in line for food, but the ladies serving the food look intimidating. They quickly slap food on my plate and move me along. I can't eat this, so I'll have to start making my lunch daily, which means I must wake up earlier. Great.

I'm looking forward to my history class, hoping my teacher will be as excellent as Mrs. Quinn. However, upon entering the classroom, I realized this teacher is a no-nonsense type and expects her students to be focused. While sitting behind a girl named Hillary, I noticed the pleasant scent of her perfume, which reminded me of sunflowers. I was apprehensive when she asked to borrow a pencil, especially since it was the first day of school. Our teacher assigned an icebreaker assignment, and I was paired with Hillary. I was pleasantly surprised to learn that we have a lot in common, as she moved to Florida from Alabama and had to adjust to the change in culture. A single father raised her, as her mother passed away due to cancer. Despite only knowing each other briefly, Hillary and I have connected, and I am excited to have four classes with her. The more I learn about her, the more intrigued I become.

It's the end of the day, and I'm already swamped with homework for three different classes. Thankfully, some of my teachers understood since it was the first day of school. But these three assignments are already overwhelming me. My mom signed us up for the bus, so now I need to find Emmanuel. Hillary asked me if I knew where the buses were, and when we got to the back of the school, Emmanuel was there chatting with two other boys. He seemed to have had a great day. I gave Hillary the bus number, and she told me it was her bus, too. As we boarded the bus, I saw Kingston and Conner rushing to get on. They said their goodbyes when we reached the first stop and got off. I thought the next stop would be

Emmanuel and me, but then I saw Hillary getting off. "Is this your stop, Hillary?" "Yeah, I'm getting off."

I exclaimed, "Great!" and we both burst out laughing. After bidding farewell to Hillary, I noticed she was heading towards the same apartment complex as us. Since we lived in a less-than-ideal neighborhood, I wanted to make sure she got home safely. She lived on the first floor, and I wondered why I had never seen her before. Sitting alone, I realized I needed to increase my social interactions. Upon entering our home, the delicious smell of dinner cooking in the kitchen greeted me. I was starving and couldn't wait to grab a snack before dinner. I warmly greeted my mother in the kitchen and shared the details of my day, including my encounters with new acquaintances like Conner, Kingston, and Hillary. I felt confident when I spoke about Hillary, and my cheeks flushed. My mother asked what made her so special, and I confidently explained how we had many similarities. We discussed how a single father raised her, and I shared that I was raised by a single mother who lived on the first floor. After informing my mother that I had homework to complete, I headed to my room to start working.

I wish I had Hillary's phone number so I could call her. Maybe I'll get it tomorrow. After finishing my homework, my mom called us for dinner, and we talked about our day. My mom said she loves her new job, and her boss is cool. Emmanuel said he made some good friends, and, as you guys know, I made some friends too. It seems like this new beginning won't be so bad after all. I was so excited for the next day that I went to my room to pick out my best outfit to impress Hillary. I had few options but settled on my black distressed jeans, a white graphic tee, and Jordans.

Emmanuel and I were waiting at the bus stop the

following day when I noticed Hilary approaching. I turned to Emmanuel and asked, "Hey, bro, how do I look?" However, he responded casually, "Who cares, bro?" I felt a bit silly for even asking him in the first place.

As Hillary approached us, she greeted us, and I could smell her perfume. After some small talk, the bus arrived, and we waited for the next stop to pick up Kingston and Conner. They sat in the two rows in front of us, and Kingston invited us to his party. I was excited about the opportunity to meet new people, as I hadn't had the chance to make many friends yet. We arrived at school and headed to homeroom with Kingston and Conner, while I told Hillary I would see her at lunch.

I felt down because I didn't have any friends and didn't want to sit alone. Conner suggested we sit together as we made our way to the lunchroom. When we entered the cafeteria, I saw Hillary in the line. She said she would reserve a table for us. We all shared amusing stories about our experiences and teachers. It felt great to be around people who had a great sense of humor and beautiful personalities. When we left the lunchroom, we headed to our next class, and Ms. Blackman announced that we would be having a beginning-of-the-year dance. I was nervous and excited because I wanted to ask Hillary to be my date but was scared she would decline. I was also worried about what to wear. Hillary turned to me and asked if I was attending the dance. I nervously said yes, and she replied, "Good, now I won't be alone." My heart skipped a beat. She sensed I wanted to ask her but was too scared, so she took the initiative. I only had one week to prepare for the dance and wished my dad were here to guide me. Not having him here is like having a hole in my heart. I didn't know the first thing about taking a girl out.

My dad would have given me the best advice if he were here.

After school ended, I sat on the bus and overheard Conner, Hillary, and Kingston discussing their outfits for the upcoming dance. I had no idea what I was going to wear. When Emmanuel and I arrived home, my mom wasn't there, but she had sent a text saying she was working overtime and that there were leftovers in the fridge. I asked Emmanuel to do his homework so I could check it, not knowing when my mom would be back. I needed to talk to her about the dance. My mom arrived at 8 p.m., and by then, I had already fed Emmanuel, made him take a bath, and put him to bed. Since my father's passing, I consider myself the man of the house and was eager to speak with my mom. I shared everything with her at once, knowing that my anxiety can sometimes get the best of me. My mom laughed and asked me to share one thing at a time. I explained to her the upcoming dance and that I needed a new outfit.

I even offered to do extra chores and babysit Emmanuel more, but my mom, being the loving and caring provider, assured me not to worry and that she would make it happen for me. I felt guilty because I knew it would add another worry for her.

CHAPTER 2

THE DANCE

> **Living in the moment means letting go of the past and not waiting for the future. It means living your life consciously, aware that each moment you breathe is a gift.**
> **— Oprah Winfrey**

On the day of the dance, my mom dropped Hillary and me off. Hillary's dad met my mom and was pleased that she allowed us to attend the dance together. The whole school seemed to be there, dressed to impress, and I was no exception. Hillary even complimented me a few times. My mom did a great job with my outfit.

Inside the cafeteria, the DJ played the latest songs. I started dancing when he played "You're a Jerk," and the crowd went wild. No one expected the new kid to have moves like that. Hillary was rapping along to her favorite artist, Nicki Major, and knew every word.

After the dance, all the kids approached me and gave

me high-fives, telling me they were impressed with my dancing skills. When my mom picked us up, we told her all about it, and she was happy that we had a good time.

When I got home, I changed clothes and received a text from Hillary. She had a great time and was surprised that I could dance. She asked if I wanted to go to the movies with her next weekend, and I told her I would ask my mom.

After exchanging texts for a few minutes, we said our good nights. I was pleasantly surprised when Monday came around, and I felt like I finally had a place at school. Kids were approaching me as if I were some celebrity. I had no idea going to a dance could change my status so quickly. Even my teacher, Ms. Blackman, complimented me on my performance.

Conner was hosting a pool party in two weeks and had already started handing out invitations. We had all grown close, so, of course, I was going. I kept my attire simple with swim trunks, slides, and a plain white tee. Hillary asked if I had asked my mom about the movies, but I realized I had forgotten. I made up a lie and told her my mom had been working late, but I promised her that I would ask that night.

When my mom got home, I remembered to ask her. She agreed without hesitation, as long as I took Emmanuel with me because she would be working late that night.

Of course, it was a bummer because I would love to spend time with Hillary alone, but I have to take what I can get. Saturday came, and since my mom was working late, Hillarie's dad dropped us off. We let Emmanuel choose the movie, and just like I thought, he picked *Diary of a Sad Kid*. After the movie, we went to have ice cream and pizza. My mom said she would be home when we got back. When we got there, I was happy because she had left home earlier that morning, and I wanted to see how her day went before she was knocked out. She's been having late days, and it's been draining her. She never had to work like this when my dad was alive. I can't wait to be able to get a job to help her out. Surprisingly, she was wide awake and waiting for us to get home. I saw two bags on the kitchen counter; she told Emmanuel and me to open them, and it was the brand-new Jordans that had just come out that day. I couldn't believe it. She told us that's why she had been picking up extra shifts at the hospital; my mom wanted to do something nice for us because she knew it was a big move, and we were team players and not complaining. She asked about the movies, and we talked about her day before she headed for bed. She made her way to her room and closed the door. I took a picture of my shoes and sent it to Hillary, and she loved the picture; she said her dad got her the same pair. She said Spirit Week was coming up, and it would have a Twin Day, so she suggested that she and I match, and I liked the idea.

I enjoyed having Hillary as a friend. We complemented each other so well. I wore my Tommy swim trunks with matching slides and a fresh white tee to Conner's pool party. I was excited to see who would be there. I'm not as nervous as I used to be since meeting Hillary and hanging out with Conner and Kingston. My self-esteem is at an all-time high, and I've made more friends than expected. The girls seem interested in me, but I only have eyes for Hillary. However, we're just friends.

When Hillary and I got to the party, quite a few people were already there. Conners' parents went all out for this party with lots of food, candy, and drinks. They even had a DJ and set up games in case anyone needed a break from the pool. It was a great party, and everyone had a good time. I was exhausted and couldn't wait to go home and hit the sheets after showering, but Spirit Week was starting Monday, and Hillary came upstairs to help me get ready. Even though I had clothes, I didn't have a lot and felt embarrassed. After my dad's passing, we were limited to one income and a monthly check from my dad's death. I avoided making eye contact and scrolled through my friend connect list, watching all the videos from Conner's party. When I looked up, Hillary had already pulled out five outfits for me to wear during the week. I was impressed by her ability to make something out of nothing. She noticed my surprised expression and asked why I looked that way.

I told her I was surprised at how many outfits she had, considering I didn't have many clothes. She told me not to worry and that I had more than I thought. She said guys don't have patience when it comes to putting clothes together. As Thanksgiving break approached, I felt sad because my dad wasn't here during the holidays. Hillary seemed quieter lately, and I wondered if she was going through the same thing. I thought about asking my mom if Hillary and her dad could join us for dinner. I didn't want to push it, but both families were missing an important member. Hillary liked the idea, and she agreed to ask her dad. When I mentioned it to my mom, she was touched by the thoughtfulness and was happy to invite Hillary and her dad to dinner.

Leading up to Thanksgiving, we made preparations for the holiday. My mother and Hillary's father pooled their resources so that we could have a fantastic meal. My mother cooked up a feast of ham, collard greens, turkey, and her famous stuffing while Hillary's dad took charge of baking the pies. I was pleasantly surprised by how delicious his apple pie was, especially considering that he didn't seem like the baking type at first glance. As my mother always said, you can't judge a book by its cover.

Thanksgiving break was a great time for me and Hillary. We managed to finish our holiday project assigned by our teacher, Ms. Blackman. She was the only one who had given us homework over the break, but we didn't mind too much. In fact, we even managed to explore the neighborhood a bit more during our time off. I discovered that there was a Boys and Girls Club located just across the street from my house. Emmanuel, Hillary, and I decided to check it out and found a mini arcade, basketball court, computer lab, and library where you could work on your projects. We even noticed a track and field area at the back of the building, leading us to believe they had a track team.

A tall African American male approached us and asked how he could help us; he looked like a retired basketball player. He introduced himself as Coach Mike. He asked if this was our first time. I guess he could tell. We said yes, and he gave us a tour of the facilities; everything was state of the art. He even stated that they are building a part for the pool and are going to start a swim team. They already have a basketball team and a track team; he said the facility was built to keep At-Risk kids out of trouble, a safe haven for kids when their parents are working late or kids whose parents aren't around. I love to play basketball, so I inquired if he had more spots on the team; he said yes, tryouts are next week, Monday at 4.

I may not be in top form as I haven't played basketball since leaving Chicago. However, I plan to practice before I meet Coach Mike on Monday. After our basketball talk, we went to the arcade. Emmanuel was thrilled to find a computer lab there. Once we were done, we headed home, where my mom had brought some delicious Popeye's, one of my favorite meals. I shared with her my plan to try out for the Boys and Girls Club basketball team, and she was happy that I had a positive and engaging activity to keep me busy. Hillary expressed interest in the track team while Emmanuel was waiting for the pool to open so he could join the swim team. My mom expressed joy that her boys were fitting in and staying positive.

It was Monday, and the day had come for tryouts. My support system included my mother, Emmanuel, Hillary, and her father, and although my dad wasn't physically there, I felt his presence. Coach Mike put us through drills, shooting, and a five-on-five game. In the end, he announced the new addition to the team, and when he called my name, I was overwhelmed. My mom and brother hugged me while Hillary and her dad congratulated me, then headed to the back of the building to prepare for Hillary's tryouts. As she stretched, I shouted words of encouragement, and she smiled back at me. When the horn sounded, Hillary moved with the speed of a cheetah, reminding me of the talented runner Jakari Hines; they could pass for sisters with their long hair, nails, and lashes. Hillary emerged victorious and secured her place on the team. Her dad invited us all to celebrate, and we went to a new hibachi spot after showering. Seeing my mom relaxing and having fun on her day off was great.

We ate, laughed, joked, and talked about school. Our parents told us how proud they were that we were taking up extra activities to keep busy. It was a great night!

HERE COMES TROUBLE

When I got home, my mom sat in the living room with a bottle of wine. She only drinks when something is stressing her out. Hey mom, everything's alright? No, your cousin Bryson has to stay with us for a while. He's in some trouble back home, and your aunt fears for him. Tomorrow, he will arrive, and you should prepare to share your room with him. My cousin Bryson is not ordinary; he tends to get into trouble and is not a role model. He smokes, drinks, and has been caught stealing. I never engaged in any of his activities, and we are only a year apart. Last year, his mother had to get him out of the juvenile detention center for stealing petty things. I did not think my mother should have taken on the challenge, but I did not argue with her. I informed my friends Conner, Kingston, and Hillary about the situation in our group chat. They seemed excited but did not know the kind of person Bryson was. I finished my homework and left the chat.

My cousin Bryson messaged me about his upcoming trip, and I was surprised as we had just been discussing it. While I was not thrilled about his arrival due to his past troubles, my mom always said everyone deserves a second chance. Bryson was eager for a fresh start, and I welcomed the change.

The next day, my mom, Emmanuel, and I eagerly awaited Bryson's arrival at the airport. However, I suspected he was up to no good when I saw his sly grin. During the car ride home, my mom mentioned she would be going to bed early. Within an hour of arriving home, Bryson asked about a balcony to smoke, which I found unacceptable in our home. I needed to protect Emmanuel from negative influences, even from family. I reminded

Bryson that he came to us for help and that we had no issues since our arrival and would not tolerate any now. I emphasized the importance of maintaining our reputation and avoiding any damage to it. Despite his skeptical look, Bryson still went out to the balcony.

We ate a delicious breakfast of eggs, pancakes, bacon, and freshly squeezed orange juice the following day. The room was tense, but my mother broke the silence by asking how we had slept. Bryson and I didn't want to answer, but my mother cleared her throat and demanded a response. I lied and said I slept okay, while Bryson claimed he slept well as if he were innocent. Emmanuel emerged from his room, looking happy, and immediately started talking to Bryson. I knew I had to watch Emmanuel, as Bryson can be very influential. Later that day, I had a game at 4, and everyone, including Bryson, would be attending. When Bryson saw Hillary, he was ecstatic. She was dressed in distressed jeans, a camisole with a cut-off jean jacket, and some Air Max, looking as pretty as she could be. Bryson introduced himself to Hillary, and I knew then that it was a bad idea for him to come live with us in Florida. Now, she still wants to be my girl! We haven't said anything about being a couple, but I knew her first. During the game, I couldn't concentrate on anything except Bryson talking to Hillary, which affected my performance.

During the game, Coach Mike called a time-out to check on me. I couldn't tell him that my performance was affected by personal issues involving a girl, especially since I was one of his best players. Despite the challenge, I tried to maintain focus as one of the best players on our team. My dad always advised me to prioritize my mental state, so I set aside my personal situation and played my best. We won the game 25 to 18, and my mom wanted to celebrate, but I was too exhausted and needed to shower and rest. The weekend went by quickly; before I knew it, it was already Monday. My mom went to enroll my cousin Bryson in our school, but I wasn't thrilled about it. The previous situation with Hillary had made me cautious, especially regarding Bryson's bad-boy behavior, which seemed to attract all the girls. I don't dislike my cousin, but I don't necessarily approve of his actions either.

Bryson said, "My cousin A is one of the most judgmental people I know. He thinks he's better than me because he came from a two-parent home until his father passed away last year. They always had the latest clothes and shoes. I can't forget about the electronics, and I admit I was jealous because I did not know my dad, and my mom has been on drugs, messing with dudes who beat on her to make ends meet and take care of me. That's when I met one of the guys from the street named Tako, who put me in the game." He had me stealing cars and anything I could get my hands on in exchange for protection and money. Tako was one of the biggest and most well-known gang bangers and drug dealers in Chicago. No one messed with him or his gang, so I joined for this reason. They made me feel like family, the family I longed for, or so I thought, until one night, things changed, and I found myself on the run from that same gang I thought was family.

I know one of Tako's biggest secrets, and he just found out that I know now he wants me dead. My cousin A thinks I wanted to be like this, but I don't. I'm just a young, lost soul who is a product of my environment, looking for a place in life. I haven't seen or spoken to my mom in months, and my aunt doesn't even know. The last time I saw my mom, she was strung out on drugs really bad. I went around the projects asking the drug dealers and anyone else if they had seen her. But after a few months of doing that with no answers, I eventually gave up and lost hope. I haven't been to school in over a year, and now my aunt expects me to go. I can't read and barely do math, so I always skip school until they kick me out. I want to do better, but I don't want people to see me as a weakling; that's why I'm always putting up this front. The only good thing about going to school is I get to talk to Hillary. I have a major crush on her; ever since I spoke to her, I've felt she's intelligent, funny, and athletic. I'm going to ask her on a date one of these days. The last time we spoke was at Aaron's game, and she seemed to like me, too, so I'm going to shoot my shot. Aaron's been acting awkward towards me. I remember when we were younger, we would play video games together and go and shoot hoops. Now he is acting like he can't stand me, but that's life; you have to take the good with the bad.

Ever since Aaron's cousin moved in, Hilary has noticed a change in his behavior. She's unsure what's happening between them, but it's not her business. Hilary thinks Bryson, Aaron's cousin, is cool and charming, and he even asks her out on a date. However, her dad won't let her go unless Aaron comes along and says it's okay. Hilary is confused as to why Aaron doesn't like Bryson, and she plans to talk to him about it. Despite Bryson's lack of enthusiasm, he agreed to the group date because he wanted to go out with Hilary.

As Christmas break approached, I was excited about the long break. My mother asked my brother and me what we wanted for Christmas, and while I knew she couldn't afford much, I asked for an iPad. My brother, Emmanuel, had no discretion when it came to her pockets and wanted half of Walmart's electronics section. I shook my head, hoping he would comprehend our financial situation more accurately. However, I refrained from saying anything, as I knew it would upset my mother and cause her to feel uneasy.

Lately, things have felt uncomfortable between my friends and me. I believe it's due to Hillary and Bryson's relationship, which I haven't been able to handle well. They started sneaking out to see each other after we went to the movies, and it's been tough for me to come to terms with it. I've suspected Bryson of making me uncomfortable, but I've tried not to let him see it. On another note, Brittany, who was in my algebra class, has been interested in me since the second week of school. Despite her advances, I can't stop thinking about Hillary, even though it's clear that she doesn't feel the same way.

One day, I contacted Brittany to ask about her plans for the break. She replied that she had no plans, which was great news because a holiday carnival was happening soon, and I thought it would be nice to invite her as my date. After proposing the idea, I was relieved when she accepted.

I heard laughter outside and saw Hillary and Bryson. My mom came in and asked why I wasn't outside with them. I didn't want to tell her the truth, so I said I had homework. Before leaving, she mentioned she would be cooking fried fish. The sight of Hillary and Bryson made me uncomfortable, so I texted Brittany until my mom called us to eat. We sat quietly until my mom spoke, but I decided to speak up. I confronted Bryson about pursuing Hillary despite knowing I liked her. I asked why he was always the center of attention and why he was even here. I even mentioned his troubled family situation. I know I went too far, but I was so angry and hurt that my cousin was trying to take the girl of my dreams away from me. My mom smacked me so hard that my neck snapped like a green bean. She sent me to my room and said not to come out until she could cool down. I was wondering how I lost control when I reached my room.

I am highly disappointed in Aaron's recent behavior. His outburst at the dinner table was unacceptable, and I expected more from him. I understand that we're all still struggling to adjust after Dad's passing, but that's no excuse for rudeness. I was shocked by his behavior because it's nothing like him. It was as if he were a completely different person. However, I spoke to him about it, and he explained that he's afraid Bryson will take me and his little brother away from him, just like he thinks Bryson took Hillary away. I reassured Aaron that I would always be there for him, but we're all family and must support each other. I suggested he try to reconnect with Bryson because he needs us now more than ever. I encouraged Aaron to be more open-minded and to apologize to Bryson. He's a handsome and intelligent young man, and I'm sure many young girls would love to get to know him if he gives them a chance. I hope he takes my advice and puts his pride aside. I gave him a goodnight kiss and told him to stay positive. It's been a difficult time for all of us, but we'll get through it together.

This past year has been quite a ride for my family, with my father's passing and our move to Florida. Adjusting to our new home has been easier for me than for my brother Aaron. I've made new friends and am excited to join the Boys and Girls Club swim team. Thanksgiving and Christmas were amazing, thanks to my hardworking and supportive mom. She's taken on the responsibility of caring for our cousin Bryson, who moved in with us for reasons I'm not entirely sure of. However, I'm happy to have him here - he's a cool guy and helps me with my music and confidence. Sometimes, I struggle with feeling self-conscious about my weight, but Bryson reminds me that big guys have much to offer. As for Aaron, he's taken on a more protective role in our family since our dad passed. While I appreciate his concern, I miss the fun times we used to have. Unfortunately, the tension between Aaron and Bryson is causing stress for my mom, who works so hard for us. I can do better by being more helpful around the house and less needy. I hope Aaron and Bryson can work things out before it's too late.

CHAPTER 3

HOW TIME FLIES

> **In a world filled with hate, we must still dare to hope. In a world filled with anger, we must still dare to comfort. In a world filled with despair, we must still dare to dream. And in a world filled with distrust, we must still dare to believe.**
>
> **—Michael Jackson**

I had a great Christmas! I got everything I wanted, and my mom even surprised me by upgrading my phone. She also got Bryson new clothes and shoes, but he asked for jewelry, which made me angry. I wish he could spend Christmas with his own parents instead of taking over my family and friends. It may seem selfish, but I can't help how I feel.

As I was leaving my room, I ran into Bryson. He asked if we could talk, and even though I didn't want to, I agreed to hear him out. He said he knows I don't want him around and that I think he's trouble, but he wants to change. He wants to learn, get good grades, and have the love and support my family and brother give me. Unfortunately, he feels like he's just another statistic. I don't know if I should trust him or not.

Although your family only has your mother, she works tirelessly for all of you. My mother used to do the same, but now she's nowhere to be found. So please don't judge me until you understand my struggles. I have no idea who my father is; my mother is nowhere to be found, and I don't know if she's dead or alive. I have been on my own for years, and it's not a good feeling to be alone in this world. He said all he needs is a chance. When I saw my cousin, I realized he was genuine. Perhaps I had been too harsh on him since he arrived; I only saw him as a problem. Bryson, you don't have to be a stereotype; you can prove everyone wrong, and I'll help you. I'll assist with your studies and even tutor you to improve your reading skills. Ultimately, we're family, and we must support each other. From today onwards, any negative feelings towards B are gone. I had no idea he was going through so much; I thought we had it tough. Boy, was I mistaken!

Since my conversation with Aaron, our relationship has improved tremendously. It felt great to have an open dialogue, and we continue to communicate more frequently. Aaron has even been tutoring me, and my grades have significantly improved. I am proud of my progress and grateful for my cousin's willingness to put his pride aside and help me.

I also have a great friendship with Hillary, although her father is somewhat skeptical of me. I understand this is normal, but I am glad Hillary is supportive and understanding. She is smart and cool, and I appreciate her assistance with homework when Aaron is busy.

Overall, things are looking up for me, and I believe my past is behind me. On Saturday, Aaron, Emmanuel, Eric (a friend from school), and I played a game of 2-on-2 basketball. Eric and I connected instantly, and it was surprising to learn that he has four younger sisters and a mother who works three jobs to provide for them. After the game, we made plans to compete again next weekend. Aaron and Emmanuel were boasting about their victory, but we are ready for a rematch.

I checked my phone, and my eyes nearly popped out of my head. It felt like I had swallowed a rock when I read the message:

"I'LL FIND YOU; YOU CAN'T HIDE"!

I'm in a tough spot now. It seems like they've found me. I'm unsure if I should contact my aunt or Aaron for help. I don't want to put anyone in danger because of my problems. I'm still trying to locate my mom, and I'm in Miami. To make things worse, someone who used to be my friend but is now my enemy is texting me. I'm not sure what to do next. My day started well because my cousin is doing well, but now I feel overwhelmed. I don't want to bother my aunt with this issue, and I'm not sure if Aaron would understand. He already thinks I'm a troublemaker. I'm so stressed out and need to talk to someone, but I don't know who to confide in. No one knows my history or where I'm headed. I have no idea what will happen next.

I am extremely preoccupied with the current situation, which has occupied my thoughts for the past 48 hours. I sincerely appreciate the hard work my aunt is putting into taking care of all of us. My cousin is also doing his best to support me in achieving my goals and creating a better future for myself. Unfortunately, my past mistakes are now causing trouble for my family. I am very nervous and scared and can't stop thinking about it. I desperately need help. I hope my family doesn't notice how much this is affecting me. I have been keeping to myself at school and rushing home as soon as the bell rings. I am constantly looking over my shoulder and crying every day. They say men shouldn't cry, but I can't help it. I hear the door opening, and I quickly pretend to be asleep so Aaron doesn't see me like this.

Upon entering the room, I noticed Bryson turn his head as if asleep. However, I knew he couldn't have fallen asleep that quickly. Lately, something has been bothering him, and he's been nervous and jumpy since receiving a message a few days ago while we were hanging out. I don't want to pry, but I hope he comes to me soon. I don't want him to think I'll judge him because he's shown me that appearances can be deceiving. I'll see Hillary and see if she knows anything.

Finally, Aaron leaves the room, says Bryson. I'm curious if he's suspicious. I can only keep this up for a bit longer. I need to confide in someone. Suddenly, the door slams, and Bryson hears Emmanuel screaming. I rush over to see what's wrong. "Emmanuel, what's going on? Why are you screaming?" "I did it...I did it!" "You did what?" "I made the swim team!" "That's fantastic! I'm so proud of you!" "Where's Aaron?" Emmanuel asks. "I'm not sure Bryson says. Why don't you try calling him?"

Emmanuel calls Aaron and shares the great news. Now I know he's coming home to congratulate him face-to-face, which means I must face him. What will I say, and how do I start the conversation? Not even fifteen minutes later,

Aaron and Hillary run through the door, yelling and screaming like Emmanuel.

After they finished screaming, Aaron and Hillary asked if I wanted to hang out. I wanted to say no but didn't want them to question me, so I said yes. I'm screaming inside, and I don't think anyone knows how dead I feel. Ever since that text, I have wanted to take my life this way; no one can get hurt, and I can feel free. I feel so trapped; this was supposed to be my way out. At least I felt free for a few months, like a typical teenager. I wonder if anyone else thinks like me. Taking my life isn't the best answer, but what else can I do? Life keeps giving me lemons, and I'm tired of lemonade. I have never felt so alone; although I have my family, I still feel alone. My aunt has something that will give me peace. While everyone is out, I will make the best of my time.

Hey Hillary, I need to head back home. I'm getting a bad feeling about Bryson; he's acting a bit strange. I'll let you know when I'm on my way. On my walk back, I saw Emmanuel and his friends but no sign of Bryson. This made me even more uneasy. When I got to the door, I found it locked and latched. I yelled for Bryson but got no response. I started to panic and banged on the door, hoping someone would hear me. Emmanuel came to my aid, and we tried to break down the door together. Hillary's dad arrived and helped us finally get inside. Once in, we found Bryson lying on the floor with a medicine bottle beside him. I shook him, and Emmanuel brought water, but he still wouldn't wake up. Hillary's dad called 911, and I contacted my mom, but she didn't pick up. She's probably with a patient, and I'm worried about how she'll take the news if Bryson doesn't pull through.

My thoughts are jumbled, I can't speak, and my tears blur my vision. Dear Universe, Father, guide us through this challenging time and help Bryson recover, even if it's for my own selfish reasons. We need clarity and direction. I never imagined he would do something like this, as I always saw him as strong and confident. Mental health issues seemed to affect other families, not ours. If Bryson pulls through, I promise to seek help alongside him. Thankfully, the ambulance arrived, and they took Bryson. As a minor, I couldn't accompany him, so Hillary's dad drove Emmanuel and me to the hospital. As we made our way, I stared out the window, lost in thought about my father. Would he have been able to prevent this? What advice would he have given me? I wonder what Emmanuel is feeling right now. My mind is racing, and we haven't even arrived at the hospital yet.

Today was supposed to be a big day for me, but now I feel confused and hurt. I thought everyone was supportive, but Bryson has been acting differently. I had noticed some changes in his behavior, but I thought it was just a phase. In our household, we communicate our feelings and thoughts so we don't feel alone. It's not always easy, but it's necessary. We use affirmations and journals to help us process our emotions. Although I don't use my journal as much as Aaron does, I find it helpful when I do. We should have encouraged Bryson to do the same. I think it could have helped him. I can tell that Aaron is stressed and thinking about our dad. He's trying to be strong for everyone since Dad isn't here anymore. My heart goes out to him.

CHAPTER 4

ARE WE ADJUSTING?

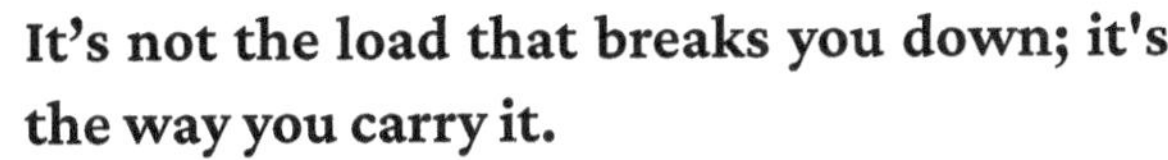

It's not the load that breaks you down; it's the way you carry it.
— Lena Horne

I have been pulling so many doubles to ensure everything goes right for this surprise vacation to Orlando that I have planned for the boys. We have all been through so much, and it's a well-needed trip. I've noticed Bryson has been a little off lately, but I don't want to push him to talk.

I'm sure he has all sorts of things running through his head, especially his mother. Bryson doesn't know it, but I still have resources in Chicago that I use to try and find my sister, but the last time I heard, she was strung out on drugs bad. My sister needs to be found so I can get her the help she needs to be the mother Bryson needs. He has been through enough, and so has she; before someone gave my sister bad drugs, she was a preschool teacher doing well for herself and Bryson. Man, how the tables can change so quickly! My co-worker Robert snapped me out of my thoughts; this guy was persistent. He kept asking to take me and the boys out, but I think it was too much too fast. He seems incredible, but the only man I know is my late husband; we were high school sweethearts, and we were inseparable until his untimely death.

Hey there, what are you up to? Oh, Robert, you're quite the joker. You're a great guy and a fantastic co-worker. But when Robert asked me out, I had to decline. I don't think it's wise to date co-workers. The truth is, I'm scared of dating, starting over, and moving too fast with someone new. Robert understood and suggested we start as friends and take things slow. We could even bring our kids along for an outing. I agreed, and we set a date. I can't wait to see my boys and relax after this hectic week. Gotta get back to work now. See you later!"

CALLING ALL SUPPORT, PLEASE COME TO THE FRONT

I'm not sure what's going on, but it looks like it will be another long night. I tried calling the guys to give them a heads-up before heading out, but no one answered. I'll have to deal with that later. I asked Robert how I could help when I got to the front. He told me to clear the area since it was a teen, and they needed everyone's assistance. I agreed and worked to move people back. After the area was clear, we saw the rescue team arriving at a speed of 100 miles per hour with the teen inside. They quickly hooked the teen up to machines, IVs, and other equipment to the teen. I wanted to know more about the situation, so I looked at the chart and saw the name. Suddenly, I froze and couldn't move. Robert had to call my name to snap me back to reality. I couldn't believe it was Bryson. I kept thinking it couldn't be him, but if it was, where were Aaron and Emmanuel?

"My nephew is the patient, Robert! Bryson is the patient who arrived," I assured Katrina that we would take care of him. Despite her concern, I reminded her that we would provide Bryson with the best possible care. Katrina attempted to help by heading to the ER, but I advised her against it, as her condition prevented her from doing so. In response, Katrina became increasingly emotional, crying out and expressing her distress. In an effort to console her, Robert softly asked how he could help. Just then, Aaron, Emmanuel, and Hillary arrived, prompting Katrina to run towards them and asking urgently what had happened. They were unable to speak and instead cried alongside her.

Meanwhile, Bryson was being treated in a nearby room, with Katrina yelling out that he was her nephew. In the waiting area, we could hear her screams and cries. Security was called to remove her from the room, and a few minutes later, my mother arrived, escorted by hospital security. She implored Katrina to let the surgeons and staff work on Bryson and to wait patiently for updates.

We have been waiting for hours, but no one has come to talk to us yet—some of my mom's colleagues who work as nurses have come out to sit with us. I can see the toll this is taking on my mom; she hasn't stopped crying. The more she cries, the more we try to hold it together. We need answers. It's already 10 o'clock, and Hilary's dad is offering to take us home. He doesn't want my mom to drive because she's in no condition, but she's refusing. "Mom, you need to come home, even if it's just to bathe and rest a little. You've been here for 48 hours. Please come with us and get some sleep." But she insists on staying to make sure Bryson comes through. I feel helpless and don't know what to do. That's when I realized I needed to speak to my mom's charge nurse, Mrs. Smith. Aaron finds her and breaks down, asking for help to get my mom home. Mrs. Smith agrees to talk to my mom, Katrina and suggests that she sleep in the nurses' quarters while keeping her updated on Bryson's progress. As we were leaving, the doctors came out and gave my mom an update on Bryson.

My mother received news from Mrs. Smith that Bryson is receiving psychiatric care for the next 48 hours. He had his stomach pumped and is now receiving medication and fluids to help him with his condition. My mother feels a bit relieved and has asked her co-worker Robert to care for Bryson while she goes home to rest. We have arrived back home and are preparing for bed. I haven't written in my journal for some time, and I believe now would be an excellent opportunity to do so.

JOURNAL ENTRY

The car ride home was completely silent. No one spoke, and the silence was so profound that you could hear a pin drop. I'm unsure how this situation will affect our family and how we'll deal with the problem. I'm scared and don't know how I'll help Bryson. Maybe we need to see someone together as a family to get through this and heal. I've never known anyone who's had to face depression or such pain, except for the loss of a loved one. What if I could create a club to help people in need, like Hillary, Bryson, and myself? I could call it "The Safe Space." I'll pitch the idea at school this week in Peer Counseling. Now, I think it's time to rest because I don't know what tomorrow will bring.

After completing my morning meditation and affirmations, I told Emmanuel we needed to hurry up and catch the bus. We left the house without discussing what happened the day before and tried to act normal. We went to school, but it was strange not seeing Bryson or Hillary at the bus stop. I couldn't concentrate on anything and wondered how Emmanuel was doing. When I saw my friends, Kingston and Conner, they asked where Hillary and Bryson were. Someone told us they didn't come to school because they had a long night out. I felt angry but didn't want to show it since they didn't know what happened to Bryson. Instead, I played it off and tried to act like everything was okay.

As we were on our way to class, I texted my mom to check on Bryson's condition. It took her around fifteen minutes to reply, and during that time, I became more distracted and unfocused than my teacher noticed. When her response finally came, my heart sank. I was still uncertain if it would be good news or bad news. She mentioned that Bryson was in and out, and his condition was touch-and-go. Hillary and James had been with him for most of the day. My mom urged me to focus on my class and reassured me that everything would be alright. This made me feel better, and I could make it through the rest of the day. Later, Emmanuel and I decided to clean, cook dinner, and visit the hospital. When we arrived, we met my mom, but unfortunately, Bryson had just been moved to the ICU and was not allowed visitors. So, we shared dinner with my mom and kept her company until her shift ended. At around 11 p.m., we returned home to prepare for the next day.

It's Wednesday, and I can only focus on getting through the day while wondering how Bryson is doing. When we arrived at school, I headed over to Mr. Hill's peer counseling class. I aimed to pitch him the idea for "The Safe Space."

"Mr. Hill, can I speak to you quickly"? Sure, Aaron, what's going on?"

"Well, I was thinking about starting a club and maybe expanding it to a podcast if it goes well." "Okay, what kind of club will this be, and what will it entail?"

Well, it's for students who may have mental disorders, loneliness, pain, isolation, or anything that makes them feel alone.

"Wow, that's a very unique club. Do you think you will have a lot of students join?" "I'm not sure, but I want to see who I can help."

"I will see when we can schedule the first meeting once you create sign-up forms and posters."

After parting ways with Mr. Hill, I began brainstorming ideas for a slogan and logo for our club. I felt a surge of excitement that rivaled the feeling of making the basket-ball team. Conner approached me, noticing my recent distance. He pointed out that Hillary seemed distracted, and Bryson had been absent or uninvolved. My best friend, Conner, urged me to be honest about what was happening. I acknowledged that it had been a hectic week but assured him I would share everything with him and Kingston in just a few days.

I had a minute to spare, so I checked up on Hillary. When I called her, she cried and asked me to come over after school. The day seemed to drag on forever, and I just wanted it to end. It was going so slow that all I could hear was the tick-tock of the clock. About 20 minutes later, the class finally finished. Since I had to work on our Safe Space Club documents, I started it last night and finished the rest in class. I had everything ready for the club's logo, slogan, and blurb, so I dropped it off at Mr. Hill's class and went to look for Emmanuel. I finally found Emmanuel waiting for me by the bus loop. On the way home, I told Emmanuel I would go see Hillary once we got off the bus. I told him I wouldn't be long, and he could call me or Hillary's phone if he needed me. As soon as I arrived, Hillary suggested we take a walk. She seemed different since Bryson's accident, and I was worried about her. I asked why she was out of school and if everything was okay. Hillary responded I have been in a dark place since Bryson. It took me back to a dark time in my life. She said that once she lost her mother, she became very depressed and was stuck in that place for a while. The struggle was so real that she even wrote a note to her dad about taking her life. This is a battle for several people, but no one wants to discuss it. Having this club at the school is needed. I am so happy that she trusts me enough to confide in me and that I could be there for her and help her through it.

"What? When did you plan this?"

"It was about two years ago. I was in so much pain from my mom's death, and I had no one to talk to."

"You have your dad."

Yes, I have my dad, but it's not the same as not having a mom. Don't get me wrong, I don't know what I would do without my dad. But it's different. My father had difficulty communicating with me about girl-related topics, as he was a man and I was a girl. We both felt lost, confused, and scared after my mother's passing. "I'm sorry I can't do much but be a listening ear, Hillary," Hillary said. Bryson's actions hit close to home and brought back unpleasant memories and pain I thought I had overcome.

However, I have started a group that could benefit you and others. It's called "The Safe Space," and it aims to support individuals experiencing similar challenges. I have attached the logo, slogan, and a brief group description. Please let me know your thoughts. Would you be interested in serving as the Vice President of this group? It would be an excellent opportunity to help others while working through your issues. Together, we could make a positive impact and overcome our tough times.

I think it's a fantastic idea that could benefit many of us who tend to keep things to ourselves, such as Bryson and myself. My father and I will be heading to the hospital shortly. Would you like to join us? "Certainly, we'll start getting ready now." "Should we prepare dinner before we leave?" "Absolutely!" It would be great to have food at the hospital. Don't forget to bring your work with you since you missed a few days. We can work on it while we visit. "By the way, I missed having you around these past few days." "I missed you too." "Alright, I'll leave you to prepare. Once we finish everything, we'll head down." "That sounds like a plan." "Remember, we need to get there before visiting hours are over." "Yes, I'm aware. We'll be quick, so don't worry."

CHAPTER 5

MAKING IT WORK?

> **At some point, we will all encounter hurdles to gaining access and entry, moving up, and conquering self-doubt, but on the other side is the capacity to own opportunity and tell our own story.**
>
> **– Stacey Abrams**

It's been touch-and-go with Bryson for the past few weeks. I have been working my doubles to help get Bryson back on his feet. Therapy has been rough; as Bryson opens up, he shuts right down. Some days are better than others, not only with Bryson but also with me. I hadn't had a good night's rest for over a month since I was working doubles when this happened—these past couple of days had me on my knees in an ocean of tears. I haven't cried this much since the love of my life passed away. Carrying such grief at such a young age cannot be easy, and I wonder if all of this stems from my sister being in and out of his life. I don't know, but I need to understand the dynamics to help and support Bryson. Where do I start? Aaron keeps talking about seeing a family therapist; that might not be so bad. I'll look into it during my break.

It has been a challenging few weeks since Bryson was admitted to the hospital. My mother looks exhausted but refuses to take a break. She comes home only to shower, check on my brother Emmanuel and me, and then return to the hospital. However, her coworker has been kind enough to drop off food and check up on us. Emmanuel and I have been managing as best we can, although it hasn't been easy.

Emmanuel has swimming practice all next week, and I must say he's fantastic at it, possibly one of the best on his team. With basketball season almost over and our team in the finals, I have little time to practice with them. Fortunately, our coach has allowed me to practice during elective classes and lunch breaks. I need to focus on these last few games and avoid distractions, even though it seems impossible.

It has been a struggle not to spend as much time with my teammates, but I plan to let them know what's happening with my family. I hope they will understand and support me during this difficult time.

It has been challenging without Mom around as much, but I was grateful to find her at home when I arrived with great news. My brother Aaron and I walked into a delicious aroma and were thrilled to see Mom cooking. Even though she looked tired, she refused my offer to help. As she prepared dinner, I sat at the table and shared my day. After yesterday's practice, my coach told me I could make it into the Junior Olympics. I was ecstatic, and Mom was pleased with what I shared. Mom said, "I love this news, but remember, as long as your grades remain good." I assured her that they are. Before dinner, Mom reminded me to wash up and call my brother and cousin. However, as I went to fetch Aaron, my mom broke down. She is still struggling with Bryson's situation, and he's having a difficult time in therapy. Aaron suggested we speak to a family therapist or counselor to help us return to normalcy. We're doing our best, and hopefully, the next few weeks will bring improvement.

The week flew by, and it was time for Bryson to come home. It's been a month since he's been here; I cleaned the house so Mom doesn't have to raise a hand. "The Safe Space" is doing well. I have learned so much from my classmates. I never would have thought so many people I call friends had many things to share. I guess you can never judge a book by its cover.

Since Bryson scared me, I've been on high alert. I've stopped working doubles, I'm not eating or sleeping properly, and I'm just working and coming home. I thought things were going well with Bryson; he and his friends were closer, his grades had improved, and he seemed to be adjusting to his new routine. However, since the incident, I've postponed our Orlando trip. Nonetheless, we all need a vacation and a break from the chaos around us. I've been trying to find my sister in Chicago, but I've had no luck. My mother always warned us about how the streets could consume you and spit you out. There's no love out there, and it seems my sister didn't get that memo. We were once very close, but everything changed when she started dating a thug. I never saw him, but I knew he was trouble from the car he drove. He had to be a dealer or a scammer.

My sister was a brilliant teacher who taught 12th-grade algebra at our local high school. Despite her intelligence, she always seemed to make poor decisions regarding men.

I tried to caution her about one particular guy, but she dismissed my concerns and told me to mind my own business. Looking back, I wish I had pushed harder because something didn't feel right about the situation. My thoughts were interrupted when my boss, Ms. Shirley, joined me in the lounge. She asked how I was holding up, and I admitted that I was taking things one day at a time. Losing my husband last year and nearly losing my nephew had been incredibly challenging. I had hoped that moving here and starting a new one would be good for us, but now I needed clarification. Ms. Shirley reminded me that some things are beyond our control, but to effect change, we must get to the root of the problem. She advised me not to waste my energy on dead plants but to start planting new ones. She also suggested that I take a vacation since I had been working tirelessly since moving here. I had mentioned wanting to save up for a trip with my boys, and maybe now was the time to make it happen.

THANK you so much for talking with me, Ms. Shirley. You remind me of my mom. She's right, and I need to figure out what's causing Bryson's fear and running away. When I got home, Bryson was watching TV in the living room, and I asked if he was okay. He said yes, but I need to know what's happening with him. I didn't want to pressure him before, but now I need answers. "I know this is a lot for a 16-year-old, but it's important to talk about what's happening." Bryson hasn't been interacting with his friends like he used to, and his grades have dropped drastically. I'm not here to judge him but to help him. When I spoke to Bryson, I could see the pain and worry in his eyes. It's not okay to put fear in a child. We need to figure out who's responsible for this and stop them. My auntie wants to know what's happening, but I don't want to tell her. I'm trying to protect her and them. When I got that message that day, I thought killing myself would be better than living in fear. See, I know that the people after me are dangerous, and I could never unsee what I saw. What I saw wasn't supposed to be seen, so now they are after me, and I don't believe it's my fault. See, back in Chicago, I was part of a gang; I participated in many things I'm not proud of, like selling drugs. I started at 12; my mom's boyfriend introduced me to gang life. The gang became my family, and they were all I knew. How was I supposed to tell my aunt that I watched the person I looked up to kill my best friend because he stole from him? It was like nothing I'd ever seen before. I mean, yeah, I saw people die. I live in Chicago, the most challenging part, but it does something different to you when it's your best friend. When I witnessed that, it instantly shot chills down my spine. I just thought, what would he do to me if he could do this to him over 20 dollars that he used to feed his sister? I can still see the smile on his face as he shot him. He was cold, he was ruthless, and everyone feared him. Tayo stood 6'5, had tattoos everywhere, including his face, and was muscle-bound. As I looked at my aunt, I assured her I was okay but missed my mom and would tell my story when I was ready. She said she understood, but I could tell she was more determined than ever to find out who was after me.

I haven't used my phone since that day. First and foremost, I plan on changing my number this weekend. I need to move on from everything and try to regain my old self, or at least make an effort. Aaron and Emmanuel are currently at the Boys and Girls Club, and I'm considering joining them for a friendly ball game. Perhaps Hillary would like to come along, too? As I approached the door, I started second-guessing myself. But just as I was about to walk away, the door opened, and Hillary nervously asked what was happening. I explained that I wanted to go to the Boys and Girls Club and wondered if she'd like to join me. She agreed and said she'd be ready in a few minutes. While I waited for her, Hillary's father came out to check on me.

"Hey, Bryson, how are you holding up?"

"All is well. I'm trying to get back to normal."

"Sounds good. If you need anything, please let me know. Talking, hanging out—anything you need, let me know."

"Okay, I will keep this in mind. Let's go, B."

"We'll talk soon. Have fun."

Hillary and I headed to The Boys and Girls Club. It took us about 10 minutes to get to the gym, and I decided to shake a few things up by running into the gym and shouting, "Whose court is this?" My Court. Emmanuel turned and called back. Man, you're going to get stomped. You should have seen Aaron's face when he saw Hillary and me. It looked as If he missed me. Aaron ran up and said Man, you wish with this big smile on his face. No, little cuz, no wishing I'm going to kick your butt all over this court. Remember, I'm the best you've ever seen. We all laughed and started the game. After playing three games, we headed to the corner store for drinks and snacks. We joked around the entire way to the store. Man, I missed hanging out with everyone. This moment gave me some life, which I needed. Once we left the store, we headed back home to play video games and listen to music; this day was going well. I felt normal again.

I was shocked to see Bryson join us for a game of ball.

Seeing him trying to regain some sense of normalcy made me happy. I hope this positive change lasts longer than two weeks. Bryson has been through so much lately, not just this situation but also having to leave home without knowing where his mom is. On top of that, he doesn't have a dad to confide in. Saying this out loud makes me realize how wrong it was to judge him. No one should have to live like this. When my mom came home, she had a massive smile for the first time in a while. I couldn't help but wonder why. She's been stressed lately, so seeing her smile made me feel like things were finally getting back to normal.

"Hey, guys, please come and sit down. I have a surprise for you that I think you'll love." Once my mother informed us that Hillary had left to go home, we all gathered and were curious about what was happening. "Get your bags ready because we're going to Orlando for a week. I have a lot of activities planned for us to do." We were thrilled and ran to our rooms to pack up as quickly as possible. When we returned to the living room, we found Hillary had also returned with her bags packed. "Let's go!" You're coming with us too, Hillary. My dad and I will be joining you guys, and Hillary's dad assisted us in loading our things into the van. My mother thought of everything. We needed some quality family time. Although Orlando was a three-hour drive, the time flew by as we chatted and sang along to our favorite songs.

My dad and I haven't been on a vacation since my mom died. When Ms. Katrina mentioned it to my dad, I prayed, and he said yes. I couldn't keep my composure when he told me we would join them. I started jumping up and down, screaming. He told me not to tell the boys because it would surprise them. I know everyone needed this vacation, but no one more than Bryson. He has been through a lot with the situation he is dealing with. He has come a long way since that scare he gave us. He will get through with a family like ours. This weekend will provide us with the time we need to return to where we used to be. We finally arrived at the hotel, and the scenery was amazing. It looked like a theme park. I have never been to Orlando before, so this will be great. As we took the tour after checking into the hotel, the outside of the hotel did the inside of the hotel no justice; it was the bomb. We had two indoor pools; one had a water slide, the other a waterfall, and every room had a flat-screen television and a jacuzzi tub. It was AMAZING; this will probably be one of my best weekends. I can't wait to see what my dad and Mrs. Katrina have planned for us this weekend; I can only imagine.

CHAPTER 6

FAMILY FUN

> **Success isn't about how much money you make; it's about the difference you make in people's lives.**
> **— Michelle Obama**

"Mom, I just wanted to express my gratitude for this trip. We needed a break, and I'm happy you are taking some time off too. I'm excited to get to our room and relax. You mentioned that we deserved this weekend and promised a great time. But we all needed this trip and should be having a good time. You have outdone yourself, and we love you for all you do for us. Are we sharing a room?" "No, our rooms are adjacent to each other; that's even better." "Thanks for our key. Do you need us to settle in and then come to your room? Is everything okay? I'm curious to see what other surprises you have planned for us. Bryson even said you've gone above and beyond for us, and we should do something for you instead. We settled into our room and noticed the vast bathroom, which made us laugh. We're taking turns to bathe before heading to your room. Thank you again for this beautiful trip."

We headed to Mom's room. Hillary and her dad were already there when we entered. Mom said here is the itinerary for the weekend, along with the passes you will need to enjoy your two-park adventure in the park. We all were so excited that we started dancing and couldn't control ourselves. Aaron exclaimed, "Mom, you're Black Girl Magic!" We all laughed and discussed which park to visit first and which rides to try.

Since we had never been to a theme park, we all searched on our phones to make an informed decision. Personally, I didn't care which ride we went on first as long as it was high in the sky and dropped very low. I think I'm the daredevil in the family; nothing scares me, and there's no ride I wouldn't try. We had never been to a theme park, so we were all on our phones looking up what cool things it offered us and what fun we would have. We needed to decide on where to start our adventure first. As we were searching, all I could think was there was nothing I wouldn't ride on.

I just found The Adventure Park, which boasts fantastic coasters and RV rides. Let's start with this park, but what did you guys find at the other parks? Bryson mentioned more water rides at the theme park he researched, called "Orlando Splash." That could be great since tomorrow's weather is expected to be over 90 degrees. Hillary, what did you discover? She found more coasters, as well as some water and RV rides. Let's be spontaneous tomorrow and have a blast. How does that sound? Aaron suggested we base our plans on how we feel in the morning, and Bryson agreed. So, we'll decide then.

"Right now, let's go back to our room and watch some movies," Hillary said yes, and we all said goodnight. I assume our parents stayed back to finalize tomorrow's itinerary. I'm excited about tomorrow and all our planned activities.

Katrina, thank you for inviting Hillary and me on this vacation. It has been a while since we last had a getaway, especially since my wife passed away. Your kindness means the world to us. How have you been holding up? These past few months haven't been easy, but you are doing a fantastic job.

Katrina smiled at me and said that everything was well and that she was glad we could support each other during these challenging times. I then mentioned that I had some news about her sister. Initially, I hesitated to share the information, but she assured me she was okay. I proceeded to share Katrina's sister's whereabouts over the last year.

Katrina opened the newspaper and learned that her sister Kandi had been in rehab for the past year. Although she was pleased to hear that Kandi was receiving assistance, she was perplexed as to why nobody had informed her of the situation. It was troubling to think that Kandii had been alive all this time without any concern for her only son's well-being. Katrina was disappointed in Kandi for being so self-centered and unfeeling about her nephew. Despite this, she decided to concentrate on the positive aspects of the situation. Bryson, her nephew, was with her and doing well. When she returned home, she would look into Kandi's situation further.

Katrina, you'll find your sister's contact info if you flip over the paper. Tomorrow morning, I'll take the kids out for breakfast and swimming, giving you a chance to call the center. Rest up now so you'll be ready for tomorrow's activities. Katrina agreed, and I went to my room to prepare for what I anticipated would be a busy day.

I am having a fantastic time on this trip. The hotel served one of the best breakfasts I've had in a while. After breakfast, we headed to the indoor pool, which was so much fun. We showered and got ready to go to the enormous theme park. Our first ride was a giant roller coaster, and I usually wouldn't go near something like that, but I decided to be brave and try it. I was with my friends Hillary, Aaron, and Emmanuel, and we waited in line together. The screams from people on the ride were loud, and I started to feel nervous. Emmanuel was talking about how he was a daredevil, and this ride was nothing for him, which made me wish I was as brave as he was. After waiting for what felt like ages, it was finally our turn to ride. Aaron and Emmanuel sat in the front cart, and Hillary and I sat behind them. I was strapped in and feeling knots in my stomach. But there was no turning back, so I closed my eyes and held on tight.

I observed Emmanuel's reaction to the rollercoaster; he appeared to have underestimated it. I couldn't resist teasing him and jokingly called him a daredevil. Our group found it amusing, and we all laughed. The ride began slowly but soon picked up speed. There were twists, turns, and dips, which caused Hillary to scream and grab me tightly. I didn't have time to be afraid, but I could hear Emmanuel screaming as loudly as Hillary. When the ride ended, we went to collect our photo. In the picture, Little Cuz and Hillary were shown screaming with their eyes closed. Emmanuel admitted that he was scared, and we all laughed before moving on to the next ride. I enjoy spending time with these guys!

We got in line once we found the next ride; at least this

line didn't take forever. This was an RV simulator ride. I guess this would be cool. I never even heard of this before, and I didn't want anyone to look at me like I was crazy, no pun intended. I would see what it's all about once I got on. My goodness, we turned a corner, and my not-so-long line turned into an extremely long line; this line was wrapped around about four different levels. We all said; what in the world kind of foolishness is this? But we couldn't turn back from this ride. It took us about 30 minutes to finally get to the section and get in line for the ride. Emmanuel shouted, "This better be the best ride ever." Once we made it on the ride, we all could sit in the same row, which was cool. This ride had a few dips, if you can call it that, moving up, down, side to side, and around. A dip, well, I guess not. The ride was incredible; now I know what a simulator is, and I think that RV simulators are my thing. I wanted to learn more about them. On the way to the next ride, Aaron said he wanted to get something to eat, so we took a break and found this restaurant that sold the most enormous turkey wings I have ever seen. Like always, we bought and shared it, which was brilliant because we couldn't eat it alone. "Okay, we need to get to the next ride. Hopefully, the line isn't a 30-minute wait."

James and I strolled around the park while the kids enjoyed the rides. We felt too old to join in on the roller coasters, and I didn't want to waste time standing in line for a short ride. James and I enjoyed some food during our walk and had a few laughs. So far, this has been a delightful day, and I am grateful. As we were about to grab some ice cream, my phone rang, and the caller made my day even better. I started to cry, and James was confused about what was happening. I covered the phone and told him that my sister was calling me back from this morning.

I regained my composure and started asking many questions, but all Kandi could say was that she would tell me everything when we met. When can we meet? We are in Orlando and won't be back until Sunday afternoon. I can send you a ticket, and you can arrive on Sunday morning. I will let you know where the key to the house is. I will see you on Sunday. Please give me your address, but don't tell Bryson anything yet. "I want to surprise him. This will be a reunion that we will never forget, sissy."

After hanging up the phone, James asked what had happened and if she was okay. I advised him to slow down, as I, too, wanted to know more details. I have decided to send a ticket to my sister, inviting her to come to Florida. She will be at the house when we return from our trip. While I want to give her a chance, I do not want to hurt Bryson. My sister has requested that I not inform him of her visit, and I intend to honor her wishes. This approach will also prevent any potential heartbreak for Bryson if she does not keep her promise. James offered to assist in any way he could, and I am grateful for his support. Although a fleeting thought crossed my mind that I should be with James, I quickly dismissed it, as he is like family.

As the day gets later, we find the kids, and they are ready for park number two. Mind you, we have been to the park since it opened at 10 a.m.; these kids have already been to the hotel pool, and they are still going. I work on my feet all day, but this pain is different. We headed to the second park for the day, and this one had more water rides, so the kids got a chance to cool off from the Florida heat. The kids went from one ride to the next, ride after ride, and it seemed like no end was in sight. I had to take a break, so I sat next to those mist fans to get some air. James said, let's try one of these rides; we can cool off and have a little fun since we didn't ride on the other side. The kids thought it was a great idea, so we all stood in line for the ride, which took us about 15 minutes, give or take. Once we got to the front of the line, got on the ride, and finished, we were drenched from head to toe. I must admit it was lots of fun and well-needed.

James and I agreed to join the kids for a few more rides, making it an enjoyable family day filled with exciting new experiences. We rode attractions and indulged in food until the park closed. The day was so pleasant that we were reluctant to see it end, but all good things must come to a close, and so did our day. Upon returning to the hotel, we decided to take a bath and reconvene in my room for a movie night. I couldn't have asked for a better day; we had an excellent time. Let's wait and see what tomorrow holds, as it is our final day in Orlando, and we must make the most of it.

CHAPTER 7
MIXED EMOTIONS

> **Watch us walk, watch us move, watch us overcome, listen to our voices, the sway. The resilience. The innovation. The raw, unfiltered, and untouched soul we have cannot be touched.**
> **—Solange Knowles**

As we depart from Orlando, my heart is filled with hope for the next chapter of our lives. My sister is moving in, and Bryson will be thrilled to be reunited with his mom after such a long time apart. I'm equally excited to see my sister after so many years. She'll be arriving this afternoon, and we plan to savor this beautiful Sunday at our leisure. We have until noon to check out, so we'll indulge in a poolside breakfast and unwind for a few hours before venturing to the shopping outlets and heading back home. We visited over 20 outlets, and I lost track of how much I spent on the kids, but they deserve it all. Watching them have so much fun fills my heart with joy and gratitude for this moment.

I'm hoping my sister coming to Florida is a good idea, but I'm not sure how my boys will handle another member in the house. We have been through so much; our life was like a rollercoaster: my husband, moving, changing schools, Bryson, and now my sister. I hope I am doing the right thing, but who's to say what that truly is? I work so much that I haven't had time like this with my boys since the love of my life passed away. After his death, I was in a bad place mentally and physically. I never really spoke to anyone, and I know that's not the way to handle any mental trauma, but I had no time. The boys needed me, and I needed them, so I did what most people do and pushed it back and moved on—or so I thought. This trip helped me to realize I had moved on but stopped making the time necessary for the ones I love the most: my boys. As they get older, so do I, and I will never get back the time I lost, so I need to slow down and make time. Now, with my sister coming, I don't want this to be added stress on the boys or myself, so I have to plan to make the time and help my sister get a job and make this work. Making memories is essential at this age; this weekend will last a lifetime.

I was delighted to assist Katrina in finding her sister. It's always beneficial to have connections wherever you go. Although I wish our weekend trip could have been longer, it was much needed. However, it's time to return to work after all the spending. Kandi's arrival in Florida positively impacts Katrina and Bryson's lives. Having an extra helping hand wouldn't hurt either. Hillary had a blast on the trip, and I wish my wife could have been here to see the young woman our daughter is becoming. Hillary is the spitting image of her mother, and it hurts when I look at her sometimes because I miss my wife so much. I've been advised to talk to someone, but I need more time, and it's not something a man should do. However, this trip made me focus on the future rather than the past and realize how much my daughter is growing. I work too much and need to spend more time with Hillary. This trip has opened my eyes, and I must make more memories with her before she goes to college. Since summer is approaching, Katrina and I should plan a vacation to create more memories with the kids. I'll bring it up once we're back home before reality sets in again.

My mom went above and beyond this past weekend to ensure we were happy. She's always been there for us, but things were tough after my dad's passing. We could see the pain she was going through, even if she tried to hide it. Despite all of this, she's still my superhero. Our trip proves that she'll do anything to make her family happy. She sacrificed sleep and food to make it happen, and I can't wait to tell my friends all about it. My mom's heart was bigger than ever, and she let us buy anything we wanted. It's amazing to see how much she loves us. This weekend will stay with me forever, and I know I can't let my mom down. I'll do my best to make her proud every day from now on.

I am so grateful for my mom—she's the best! This past weekend, she went above and beyond to surprise us with a trip she worked doubles for months to save up for. I honestly couldn't ask for a better mom. This weekend brought out her shining personality, which was great to see after all we've been through. Sometimes, she tries to handle everything alone, but we all know that's not the best approach. However, this weekend was different—she was happy and smiling, making me feel like things were looking up for all of us. The only thing that would make this trip even better is finding out what's going on with my aunt. I know it would make my mom and Bryson very happy.

Now, let me tell you about the shopping we did! We visited over 20 stores and found some fantastic stuff. It was tiring, but every step was worth it. I even got some new shoes and clothes! My mom was just happy to sit back and enjoy every minute. Hillary and her dad are also having a great time. This trip is one of my favorite memories since moving to Florida. It's been nice to take a break from our everyday lives, and I hope we can plan something like this again in the summer. No one has a better mom than the mom that I have. She has done more this one weekend than she needed; my mom has worked doubles for months to surprise us with this trip. Wow! I couldn't ask for a better mom. This weekend put her in such a great mood. We have been through a lot, and Mom sometimes shut Emmanuel and me out and tried to handle everything alone. That didn't work out very well. It took a while for Mom to get back to normal behavior, but she has not been the same since Dad. This weekend, though, really brought out the mom in her. I knew she was happy and smiling, making me feel like things were looking up for us all.

All that's missing now is finding out what's going on with my aunt. I know finding her would make my mom and Bryson happy. Let me talk about these outlets, man. They are sick. We went to over 20 stores. I never thought I could walk so much in my life. Every step was worth it. New shoes and clothes, and Mom just sat back and enjoyed every minute. I think Hillary and her dad are also having a wonderful time. This trip is one of my best memories since moving to Florida. We need more of these getaways from our everyday lives. I hope we can do something this summer.

I'm planning a summer trip and bringing it up on the way home. This weekend was one of the best since my mom passed away. My dad was struggling after my mom's death, and we just coexisted without much communication. Have you ever felt invisible and unheard, like you're in a dark hole? That was how I felt, and all I wanted was for my dad to see me. But I realized we were both grieving and coping in our own ways. This weekend helped us both. My dad and I had a great time together. He's usually busy with work, so spending quality time with him was excellent. We went shopping, and I enjoyed it because of our time together. I needed this time, and the memories of this weekend will stay with me forever.

Today is significant for me as I will finally reunite with my sister, Katrina, and my son, Bryson. There is a lot I need to share with them, but I am not quite ready to disclose everything that has happened to me. The experiences I have been through are not ones any human should endure. I used to be an educated teacher, but I fell in love—or so I thought—with a man who made me feel like I was the best thing since sliced bread. He filled my head with so much positivity that I believed I could walk on water, and no one could convince me otherwise. My family attempted to intervene, but I shut them out, especially my sister, who tried the hardest. I was willing to do anything for this man because he made me feel incredible. However, everything changed after our trip to the islands. We arrived on a beautiful Thursday, and the sun kissed my skin; it felt like paradise.

When we reached the hotel, we didn't have to check-in. It was all taken care of, and I thought my man took care of everything, but was I mistaken? We reached the room, and two guys were already in the room. I was in shock, so I asked what was happening, and one of the guys said to sit and relax. At this point, I didn't know what to do. I wanted to run but had no idea where to go. "My man said it's okay, trust me." They made me a drink, and the next thing I knew, my man said, "I need you to do me a favor." So, of course, I said, "Anything for you," and this is where my life changed. I became a human mule carrying drugs in my body from one country to the next. One drop didn't go so well; a few bags burst in my stomach, and I became extremely sick. They rushed to one of their makeshift clinics to remove the other bags. Up to this point, I was clean; a few weeks later, I discovered I was pregnant. What am I to do? I can't carry anymore, and I don't want this life for my kid, so I stopped seeing my guy and focused on work and my baby. After Bryson was born, it was like something came over me. I don't know if it was depression or what, but it was like something was missing in my life. I always wanted something, and I couldn't understand what it was. One day, I ran into my ex, and he asked if I wanted to go out for dinner, and I said yes. He still doesn't know we have a kid together, and I was not letting him around our son. We hung out, and it was like old times; we laughed and talked, and when it was time to leave, he asked for one last drink, which was my turning point. He had to have slipped something in my drink because I cannot tell you how I got home that night or why I started calling him for more of whatever he slipped me.

My days and nights became one. I started neglecting my son. It was not bad at first, but it got worse the older he got. I became a different person, someone I was ashamed of. I couldn't recognize myself in the mirror. It wasn't good, and days became weeks and weeks became months, and so on. I owe my kid more than an apology. But what and how will I do it? I will work hard to convince him that I have changed. I'm not the same person I was a few months ago; I am better than I have been in years. It's time to board the plane. There's no turning back. Now it's time to face my sister and son.

I couldn't believe my eyes when we saw my mom at the door. I didn't know if I should be happy or angry. She left me by myself. I had to do things to survive, and now I'm on the run. When my mom saw me, she hugged me, but I couldn't move. I was like a mannequin: stiff, dull, and emotionless. She just kept apologizing, but I didn't care about that. I had questions that needed answers. I thought she was dead. I would cry myself to sleep at night because I didn't know where she was. People didn't know that I saw my mom do a lot of things growing up, and it has caused me so much trauma and resentment towards her. Everyone was staring at me as I snapped out of my thoughts. They thought I should've been happy to see my mom alive and clean again.

However, little did they know that I had already witnessed this magic show and had seen all the tricks when I attended it with my mother. Overwhelmed by the situation, I quickly retreated to my room to gather my thoughts. As I stormed off, I noticed Aaron following behind me.

"Hey, what's going on? Your mom is here; shouldn't you be happy?"

"I am happy, but I'm also mad. How can you leave your son to chase after men and drugs?"

"I understand, but she had no control over what was happening to her. She had a disease; that's what addiction is. She's here now, and everyone deserves a second chance."

"Yeah, they do, but why can't she be more like your mom? She used to be, but not anymore."

"Look, I can't answer that in a way that makes sense, but everything will work out. Let's go back out there and make the best of it.

"Yeah, you're right!"

I was taken aback by my son's strong reaction to my presence, as I never expected him to be so repulsed by me. It was heartbreaking to know that he despised me. Though I have made mistakes in the past, I am now striving to improve myself and my relationship with him. I desperately want him to comprehend this. I am incredibly grateful that my sister has taken in Bryson; he was getting into a lot of trouble in Chicago, and I couldn't provide the support he needed. I've heard rumors that he's on the run from something, but I'm not sure what that something is. My thoughts were interrupted when Bryson came over and embraced me tightly. I felt a wave of relief wash over me when he expressed how much he missed and loved me.

"Love you too, baby!"

"Mom, I apologize for my behavior. I was overwhelmed with thoughts."

"It's understandable that you may feel upset with me, but I want you to know that I have made positive changes and am committed to being a part of your life."

"Yo, man, it's real tough when you get hurt, you know? Especially by your own mom. Like, I put my trust in you, and then *bam*, you just leave. It ain't cool. It feels like a punch to the gut, worse than any fight I've ever been in.

I hope you stick around; it will mean a lot."

"I won't leave you, baby, I won't!"

CHAPTER 8
UNIFIED ONCE MORE

Family means no one gets left behind or forgotten.
—David Ogden Stiers

It's been a few months since my mother came to visit, and things are going well. I'm proud of her for staying clean for the longest time I've seen her. Hillary's dad and my Aunt Katrina helped her get a job at the elementary school down the street, giving her a sense of stability as a teacher's aide. She comes home happy, which makes old issues disappear. Aaron has been helping me process all my past pains and problems every day. It's incredible how the club he started has grown from one classroom to an auditorium. We've decided to expand to a podcast and social media, and I'm surprised that I was not the only one experiencing such pain. Talking about our problems in a safe place with no judgment feels great. It helps us cope with the daily trauma we face and realize that our problems are minute compared to other people.

As the end of the school year approaches, it's time to start thinking about summer vacation. However, I focus on ensuring I have the necessary points to advance to 10th grade. It hasn't been easy, and my grades have suffered in recent months. I may need to take some online classes to catch up, but I'll find out before the end of the school day.

Despite the challenges, I'm determined to make my aunt and mom proud, especially my aunt, who has worked hard to keep me safe and out of trouble. I owe her a lot for her sacrifice. When I walked into the guidance office, I saw Hillary was volunteering that day and she smiled and told me I had all the points I needed to move and get into my correct grade. I was overjoyed and ready for summer.

HILLARY REASSURED me that I shouldn't overthink things and that she and the staff were there to help me with any needed information. She acknowledged that I'd been through a lot and promised to do everything she could to ensure I had everything I needed to move forward. I was relieved to hear that I was on track, but I must pass all my courses with a B to move on to the next grade.

I thanked Hillary and left the office to share the good news with Aaron. I was so grateful for the support and guidance I had received and felt confident that I could achieve my goals with their help.

While walking down the hallway, I noticed Bryson running towards me, excitedly exclaiming that he was going to the 10th grade and thanking me for helping him achieve it. I asked him to slow down and explain what he meant. He said he needed to maintain all B's, and I had shown him that he could do it. Hearing this made me happy, knowing I could uplift Bryson and boost his confidence. I suggested that we ask the teachers for ways to improve his grades, and we headed off to our classes. On the way, we ran into our friends Kingston and Conner, who invited us for lunch. Unfortunately, we had to decline as we had classes to attend. I promised to invite them over to hang out after school instead.

I am grateful that things are looking up for my family. My sister is doing well by working and staying sober while the kids succeed in school. As for me, work has been going well, and Robert invited me out this weekend, which I accepted. I have yet to inform my friends, but I hope they will be happy for me. My shift will end soon, and I plan to brainstorm summer trip ideas with James and my sister. This will be good for her, just like our last trip a few months ago, which was good for us. As I was lost in thought, I was called to assist a patient, so it's back to work.

I'm still in shock that Katrina agreed to go out with me. I'm not sure how to act now that I finally got a "yes" from her. Since this family event involves teenage boys, I need to plan something they will enjoy. I'm unsure how to make a good impression on them, but I have an idea. We will go to the Zoom Room, where they have a wide range of activities such as video games, skating rinks, go-karts, laser tag, and more. I plan on arriving early to have lunch and get to know each other better before hitting the Zoom Room. It's been a while since I've been on a date, especially since my wife left me and the kids to start a new life. It was a difficult time for me, and I still feel like I haven't fully recovered. However, I owe it to my kids to be the best father I can be and give them more of me and less of the broken man that I am right now. I haven't talked to anyone about how I feel, and I'm unsure if that's good or bad. I don't want to bring negative energy into this friendship, but if Katrina and I decide to start a relationship, she deserves to know the truth. I believe this date will help me and the kids feel a sense of normalcy again.

Today was a long day, and I'm looking forward to getting home to unwind. I can't wait for the weekend to spend time with my loved ones and maybe grill some food while we watch Netflix. Spending time with them has been great, keeping me focused and on track. As a recovering addict, I attend weekly meetings to stay clean and accountable, and being in a new environment around supportive people has boosted my confidence. I'm considering returning to education, not in a traditional classroom but at a center or shelter to help others like me who may have lost their way. It's in my heart to help others avoid the same mistakes I've made. I'm not sure where to start, but I'll do some research and plan it out.

Enough about me. I'm looking forward to hearing about everyone's day at dinner tonight. It's been a long road, but I can see the light at the end of the tunnel. I'm ready to head home and get some exercise in. As I turn to leave, the principal asks if I can stay a little longer to help with after-school activities. Although I wanted to say no, I decided to stay a little longer to help out. I texted Katrina and my friends to let them know I'd be at the school until 6 p.m. To my surprise, Bryson called immediately to say he and Aaron would walk me home. I feel so lucky sometimes to have these wonderful people in my life, even if I don't always feel deserving of their love.

I had to do dry land **(exercise)** for the rest of the practice because I missed a day last week. After I finish, I need to make sure Aaron walks home with me since it will be late. The past few weeks have been great. Auntie Kandi is settling in, and she's fun to be around. I didn't know she was also a swimmer in school, and she's been giving me pointers, which is helping me get stronger in the water. We've been having family dinners every night since Aunt K came to live with us, which we haven't had in a long time, and it's back in full effect. Mom isn't working as much anymore, so she comes home at a good time, and we get to share our day and talk through any issues or concerns. This has helped all of us; we all come to the table with something to share from our day. I'm looking forward to getting home and having our family time. I must focus before the coach makes me work out the entire practice.

As I approach the house, I hear the sound of ringing bells. I know it can't be my dad, who never comes home this early. Upon entering, I find my dad dancing and cooking in the kitchen, looking happier than I've seen him since my mom. It's an incredible sight to see. I dropped my bags and joined him, and he asked if I wanted to dance with him. I accepted, and we laughed. I joked about him not hurting himself with those old moves and he said just keep up. Dancing and laughing brings back good memories. Afterward, we ate and watched TV before discussing my school and summer plans. I tell him I'll be going to 10th grade, and he congratulates me. I suggested we take a summer trip with Ms. Katrina and the guys, and my dad laughed, saying he was thinking the same thing. We shared some ideas, and I wrote them down to discuss later. Once we finished, we cleaned the kitchen and put the food away, and then we turned on some music and continued working together.

I arrived home before everyone else, so I decided to tidy

up a bit and start cooking. Since I wanted to share, I baked a homemade cake for dessert. Dinner turned out to be almost a five-course meal. I prepared chicken and shrimp Alfredo with garlic bread, soup, salad, and cake. The house smelled amazing, and I wanted to start eating, but I waited for everyone to come home. After cleaning the kitchen and getting ready, I put on some music to relax while waiting for everyone to arrive. It's after 6 o'clock, and they should be home by now. I'll give them a few more minutes before I start calling them to check up on them. Suddenly, I fell asleep on the couch and woke up to everyone walking in simultaneously. My family was curious about the delicious smell from the kitchen, so I asked them to freshen up while I set the table. We all enjoyed our meal and shared our day's experiences. Bryson is working on his grades to move to the 10th grade, Aaron's club is expanding, Emmanuel is doing even better in swimming, and Katrice is being asked to stay longer at work to help. Everyone is excited because we've been asked to go out on Saturday. Aaron even asked for seconds, and Robert asked if he could take us on a date. Bryson was thrilled, and Emmanuel was hesitant, but I explained that I had to mention my kids to Robert and that we all had to go. It was a great night, and we enjoyed each other's company.

"Okay, we could give him a chance and not judge him. What do you think, Bryson and Emmanuel?"

"We will give him a chance, Auntie."

"Okay, Mom, I'm with Aaron and Bryson; we will give him a chance."

After completing everything, we heard a knock at the door. It turned out to be Hillary and James. We welcomed them inside and offered them some cake, which they happily accepted. While enjoying the cake, Emmanuel suddenly announced that we were going on a date next Saturday. We were all surprised by this sudden announcement.

But then James said they wanted to discuss planning a summer trip together. We all agreed excitedly, as we had been thinking about it since our last trip. They shared some fantastic ideas for places to visit, and now we have to decide which one will be the best for our family. We're looking forward to this summer adventure!

I stepped away from the group to call Conner and Kingston. I remembered that I needed to speak to them after school. I wanted to invite them over to my house tomorrow. "Hey guys, I just wanted to apologize for today and the past few weeks." There have been a lot of changes in my family, and I've been neglecting our friendship." "Let's get together after school, grab a bite to eat, and play some ball." "We can go to my house." "Let me know what you guys want to do." They both said they understood and that family always comes first. "We can hang out this Friday for sure. I'll see if you guys can stay over so we can all catch up." "Sounds good. We'll chat tomorrow."

I returned to the living room, and we still needed to decide where to go. But I'm okay with whatever, as long as we're together. In the middle of my thoughts, Bryson says what I'm thinking: "Wherever we end up, it'll be great because we're together." "That's right, my thoughts exactly." Mom and Hillary looked at us like we had three heads and said, "What? "We need your opinion to ensure we are all happy on the trip." "Okay, give us until next week to research all these places and make sound judgments. This will give us time to find cool places to visit in each one of these destinations on the list. Bryson, we'll divide the list and make a presentation to present our findings. This way, everyone can see what's good in each one of these destinations on the list. Okay, how does that sound to everyone?" Everyone loved it and was on board. "Let's get to work on this project." Bryson said, "Great, we'll be working this weekend." "Yeah, but we'll make it fun while doing it. No worries, we got this." "Alright!"

CHAPTER 9

THE SEARCH HAS STARTED

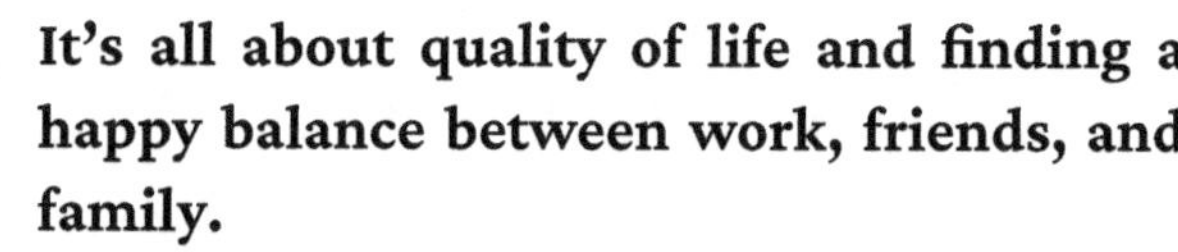

It's all about quality of life and finding a happy balance between work, friends, and family.

– Philip Green

I've been looking for B everywhere since a couple of months back; B saw me kill his best friend for stealing from me. I didn't want it to go that way, but it did. I had my soldiers looking for him everywhere, day in and day out, and he hadn't turned up. I haven't even seen Kandi in months. Both are missing, but luckily, my money and resources are long. I heard Kandi's sister Katrina and her boys moved to Florida. I don't know if that's true or not, but I have a long-time associate who is a detective there, and maybe he can help me.

The phone rings.

"Hello, my friend! It's been a while since we last spoke. How have you been?"

I understand how challenging it can be to balance

work and caring for a child. But I was hoping you could do me a favor.

What's that?

I am searching for a friend who has relocated to Florida and changed her phone number. I plan to surprise her with a visit.

"Oh, yeah, who is this person from your past relationships?"

"No, not at all. It's just someone I've known for a long time."

"All right, text me the information, and I'll get back to you. Maybe we can hang out like old times when I visit."

"Yeah. Maybe!"

After ending the call, I felt relieved knowing JMoney would handle everything. We used to run the city together in our youth, but he chose a different path. I understand his decision, as he had to take care of his daughter after his wife passed away. It's a responsible move for a father. As I snapped out of my daydream, Tony entered and informed me that he couldn't locate B but found one of his associates. I instructed Tony to bring him in, hoping he could provide some information about B's whereabouts. "Hey, have you seen B around?" I asked the associate. "I've been searching for him everywhere."

I don't know where he is; however, he had a packed bag and was on his way to the airport.

"Do you know where he went?"

"Yes, he mentioned that his aunt had sent him a ticket. Thanks for the info, soldier."

I peeled off a fresh $100 bill and gave it to the child. Tayo always looks out for children. "Hey, treat yourself to something nice."

"Thank you so much, Tayo."

I took out my phone and messaged JMoney with the details. I requested all the information about this auntie. JMoney replied with a thumbs-up emoji. Even though I knew Kandi had a sister, I never had the chance to meet her family. They were pretty snobbish and pretentious, which I didn't have the patience for. Kandi and I had an on-and-off relationship, and when she got pregnant, she vanished until her child was two; I watched the child grow up. I was a hero to the neighborhood kids, but some people saw me as a monster. And I admit that I did some monstrous things, but only when I was pushed to the limit. I'm eager to leave this life behind, but I can't do that as long as B holds that secret over me. I must leave this game with a clean slate and nothing hanging over my head. That's why I need to deal with B.

I informed my team that I was taking the day off and drove home in my 2022 BMW 750LI. I was waiting for JMoney to send me some information so I could catch the next available flight. While waiting, I decided to pack an overnight bag as I wouldn't need to stay for long. I took the initiative to book a ticket and a hotel a few weeks in advance, just in case. This wasn't the life I had envisioned for myself, but it was the one I had been dealt with, and now I was determined to live it without fear or uncertainty. I longed for a family to love and care for; I would be different if I had one. With them, I wouldn't have to worry about anything. Maybe someday I'll have a family and live the life I've always wanted. JMoney finally sent me an update, and I'll be leaving in a week.

Summer has finally arrived after what seemed like a long wait. A few weeks ago, we went out with my mom's friend Robert and his kids; they are all great people. We plan to hang out more with them when we return to town.

As for our trip, we decided to go on a cruise to explore multiple places and see different things. None of us have ever been on a cruise before, so we're excited to experience it. We've finished packing and are ready to head to the port. My mom and auntie don't need any help, but Bryson and Emmanuel are outside, ready to go. It's just a week-long trip, but these ladies are packing as if it's a year! Despite that, I'm excited about this trip and know we will have a fantastic time.

It's scorching and humid outside, and I feel like my skin is melting off. I've been waiting for about 20 minutes, and the only one who's ready is my cousin Emmanuel, but I'm not sure if that's a good thing. "Hey, cousin," I ask, "do you have everything you need?" He replies with a casual

"Yeah, you think I'm slow?" I continue, "Okay, do you have your toothbrush, swim trunks, tee-shirts, and..." He suddenly runs back into the house, unsure what he forgot, but it's okay. This will be my first cruise and trip with my mom, and I'm excited for what's to come. I've been dreaming of a day like this, and now it's finally here, and I'm on edge with anticipation. I can't wait to board the boat and enjoy the all-you-can-eat food and music all day. Plus, I can rest on the deck without worrying about anyone stealing from me. This is going to be an epic trip. Yes, I said "Epic."

We arrived at the port with 20 minutes to spare and checked in before heading to our room. The doors made it seem small, but it turned out to be a spacious cabin with a living room, dining room, and even stairs. I asked my mom how we managed to get such a large cabin, and she explained that we paid for a suite because we were always together. It made sense, and I was excited to explore and relax. The balcony offered a calming view of the water that

I knew would be my favorite spot. After check-in and onboarding, we all went to eat before hitting the pool. The boat had already started moving, and everyone enjoyed the cool breeze and beautiful pool. Hillary and the guys couldn't get enough of the slide, so I joined the fun.

This week has flown by quickly; we have been to three countries, and each was an experience of a lifetime. Having my family enjoy themselves is the best feeling in the world. The smiles are more significant than our first trip, and that's saying a lot. Cruising might be the thing for us. I'm looking forward to returning to dry land; and walking normal again. James and Hillary are enjoying themselves. James is doing a great job being present and giving her space when she needs it. Reconnecting with my sister has been great. She's very energetic and keeps up with the guys while I'm relaxing; she is out having a grand old time with the kids. We will dock back home in the morning. According to the agenda, we can leave our rooms at 6 a.m. I would love to be the first off the boat, but if I know the kids, they will want the opposite. I work tonight and should have taken the day off, but I had not thought about it until now. It will work itself out; I am not going to over-think it. My sister snapped me out of my thoughts and asked me to join them since it was the last day of the trip. Now, here I go, getting in this water, and I can't swim. I'll stay on the edge of the pool and kick my feet.

Bryson and I needed this trip. We've never been on one before, and while I know it doesn't make up for what I've put him through, it's a start. I've been so energetic on this trip, doing activities like zip-lining with the kids and going down the slide a thousand times. It's been nonstop, and I'm loving it. We'll return to reality tomorrow, but I don't have to work until next week. I offered to help in the front office for summer school and registration. I plan to hang out with the guys at the pool this week. I'll invite Hillary to join us since she's always around. She's like a little sister to me but without the fighting. It's time to dip in the pool and chat with Katrina.

I have been having a fantastic time on this trip with Hillary. Our bond has been growing stronger, and I hope it continues. Being a single father is challenging, especially for someone like me who used to lead a different lifestyle. But I made the necessary changes to prioritize my family and provide for my daughter. I won't let her down. Spending time with Katrina and her family has been a breath of fresh air.

I'm excited to go home and plan my next trip. I didn't realize how much I needed a break to enjoy life until now. I'm grateful to Katrina for reminding me of its importance. "Good morning, family! It's time to wake up and prepare to leave the boat. Unfortunately, we can't stay longer because I have work tonight." "Katrina, why didn't you take the day off?" "I forgot and can't find a replacement on such short notice."

Nevertheless, we need to get ready and leave. It took us around 20 minutes to exit the boat, but we finally made it. I'm happy to be heading home and getting some rest. Once we arrived, we chatted and laughed about our next trip. James kept urging us inside, but I didn't understand why. When I opened the door, Kandi screamed, Bryson cried, and I was confused about what was happening.

James yells, surprised, "Who are you, and why are you in my home?" I turn around and reply, "I don't know this man. What's happening, Kandi?" Bryson seems terrified, and suddenly, the man pulls out a gun. "Thanks, old friend... What does he mean? You know him, James?" I am still trying to figure out what's going on.

"Yo, what are you doing pointing that gun at B? You said you wanted to meet up with an old friend. Yes, these are my old friends. What is going on in my home? I am not happy, James. You brought trouble into my house with my boys."

We need to stop talking, B. You know what needs to be done."

"Hold on, Tayo. My son won't be going with you."

If he doesn't come with me, the situation with your family may become unpleasant.

"Tayo, I cannot allow you to do that. I would never have assisted you had I known your intentions. Well, old friend, I have to do what needs to be done. Let's go, B, now."

"You will not take my nephew anywhere. This ends today. What does he owe you, and I will take care of it? Spit it out. You invaded my home and terrified my family; this ends today."

Today, my issues with Bryson will end once I take care of him, Katrina.

"No, Tayo. This ends today. You will not lay hands on my son. I am not the same person I used to be.

Kandi, please get out of the way. No! Are you willing to kill your son? What? What are you saying, Kandi?

THE SHOCKER

Everyone stood there, confused. Kandi looked Tayo in the

eyes and said, "Yes, he's your son." Tayo lowered the gun and asked Kandi, "Why didn't you tell me?"

Katrina turned to James and said, "I'm confused about how this man got into my house."

James responded by apologizing to Katrina. "Katrina, I'm sorry. He told me he knew you, and I was trying to help a friend. All I know is that my friend reached out to me and said he needed help, and I thought I was doing a good thing."

Katrina tells James to leave, saying she never wants to see him again. Hillary shouts why are we mad at each other? This guy is the enemy. Katrina responds and tells Hillary she doesn't understand and that they will talk later.

"Later, you told my dad you never want to see him again, which also includes me, right?"

"No, that doesn't include you. Can we please talk about this later?"

As James tries to leave, Bryson enters the room, pointing a gun at Tayo. "No, Bryson" yells Kandi.